BASKETBALL LEGENDS

Kareem Abdul-Jabbar
Charles Barkley
Larry Bird
Kobe Bryant
Wilt Chamberlain
Clyde Drexler
Julius Erving
Patrick Ewing
Kevin Garnett
Anfernee Hardaway
Tim Hardaway
The Head Coaches
Grant Hill
Juwan Howard
Allen Iverson
Magic Johnson
Michael Jordan
Shawn Kemp
Jason Kidd
Reggie Miller
Alonzo Mourning
Hakeem Olajuwon
Shaquille O'Neal
Gary Payton
Scottie Pippen
David Robinson
Dennis Rodman
John Stockton
Keith Van Horn
Antoine Walker
Chris Webber

CHELSEA HOUSE PUBLISHERS

KOBE BRYANT

Robert Schnakenberg

Introduction by
Chuck Daly

CHELSEA HOUSE PUBLISHERS
Philadelphia

Produced by Combined Publishing, Inc.

CHELSEA HOUSE PUBLISHERS

Editor in Chief: Stephen Reginald
Managing Editor: James Gallagher
Production Manager: Pamela Loos
Art Director: Sara Davis
Director of Photography: Judy L. Hasday
Senior Production Editor: Lisa Chippendale
Publishing Coordinator: James McAvoy
Cover Design and Digital Illustrations: Keith Trego
Cover Photos: AP/Wide World Photos

The Chelsea House World Wide Web site address is
http://www.chelseahouse.com

First Printing

1 3 5 7 9 8 6 4 2

Library of Congress Cataloging-in-Publication Data
  Schnakenberg, Robert.
    Kobe Bryant / Robert Schnakenberg ; introduction by Chuck Daly.
      p. cm. — (Basketball legends)
    Includes index.
    Summary: Discusses the personal life and basketball career of the guard
  for the Los Angeles Lakers who became the youngest player in the NBA in 1996.
    ISBN 0-7910-5005-X
    1. Bryant, Kobe, 1978-   —Juvenile literature.   2. Basketball players—
  United States—Biography—Juvenile literature.   3. Los Angeles Lakers (Basketball
  team)—Juvenile literature.   [1. Bryant, Kobe, 1978-   . 2. Basketball players.
  3. Afro-Americans—Biography.]   I. Title. II. Series.
  GV884.K794   1998
  796.323'092—dc21
  [b]   98-31349
                                                                        CIP
                                                                         AC

CONTENTS

Becoming a
Basketball Legend

Chuck Daly

What does it take to be a basketball superstar? Two of the three things it takes are easy to spot. Any great athlete must have excellent skills and tremendous dedication. The third quality needed is much harder to define, or even put in words. Others call it leadership or desire to win, but I'm not sure that explains it fully. This third quality relates to the athlete's thinking process, a certain mentality and work ethic. One can coach athletic skills, and while few superstars need outside influence to help keep them dedicated, it is possible for a coach to offer some well-timed words in order to keep that athlete fully motivated. But a coach can do no more than appeal to a player's will to win; how much that player is then capable of ensuring victory is up to his own internal workings.

In recent times, we have been fortunate to have seen some of the best to play the game. Larry Bird, Magic Johnson, and Michael Jordan had all three components of superstardom in full measure. They brought their teams to numerous championships, and made the players around them better. (They also made their coaches look smart.)

I myself coached a player who belongs in that class, Isiah Thomas, who helped lead the Detroit Pistons to consecutive NBA crowns. Isiah is not tall—he's just over six feet—but he could do whatever he wanted with the ball. And what he wanted to do most was lead and win.

All the players I mentioned above and those whom this series will chronicle are tremendously gifted athletes, but for the most part, you can't play professional basketball at all unless you have excellent skills. And few players get to stay on their team unless they are willing to dedicate themselves to improving their talents even more, learning about their opponents, and finding a way to join with their teammates and win.

It's that third element that separates the good player from the superstar, the memorable players from the legends of the game. Superstars know when to take over the game. If the situation calls for a defensive stop, the superstars stand up and do it. If the situation calls for a key pass, they make it. And if the situation calls for a big shot, they want the ball. They don't want the ball simply because of their own glory or ego. Instead they know—and their teammates know—that they are the ones who can deliver, regardless of the pressure.

The words "legend" and "superstar" are often tossed around without real meaning. Taking a hard look at some of those who truly can be classified as "legends" can provide insight into the things that brought them to that level. All of them developed their legacy over numerous seasons of play, even if certain games will always stand out in the memories of those who saw them. Those games typically featured amazing feats of all-around play. No matter how great the fans thought the superstars were, these players were capable of surprising the fans, their opponents, and occasionally even themselves. The desire to win took over, and with their dedication and athletic skills already in place, they were capable of the most astonishing achievements.

CHUCK DALY, now the head coach of the Orlando Magic, guided the Detroit Pistons to two straight NBA championships, in 1989 and 1990. He earned a gold medal as coach of the 1992 U.S. Olympic basketball team—the so-called "Dream Team"—and was inducted into the Pro Basketball Hall of Fame in 1994.

1

THE NEXT MICHAEL

The crowd had come to see a battle for the ages. The 1998 NBA All-Star Game had everything—the world's greatest players and New York City as its stage. But the 18,323 people assembled in Madison Square Garden were also there to see the NBA's present going toe to toe against its future. Michael Jordan and Kobe Bryant were going one-on-one.

Kobe got the party started early. Midway through the first quarter, he hammered home an incredible 360-degree dunk that brought the celebrity-filled Garden crowd to its feet. Jordan responded immediately, drilling two jump shots in the 19-year-old Bryant's face. You don't have to dunk to get on the highlight films, Jordan seemed to be saying to the kid everybody was touting as "the next Michael."

The contest continued throughout the evening, with each man trying to top the other's heroics.

During the 1998 NBA All-Star Game, this is what the crowd had come to see—the match-up of Michael Jordan and Kobe Bryant.

Michael Jordan attempts to shoot over the reach of Laker Kobe Bryant. Kobe has been called "the next Michael Jordan."

Late in the third quarter, Bryant sprinted down court on a fast break. Using his left hand, he wrapped the ball behind his back to fake a pass and soared to the hoop for a fallaway scoop layup. The impossible shot splashed through the net and again drove the capacity crowd into a cheering frenzy. Two possessions later, Bryant drained a three-pointer to pull the Western Conference team within 12 points of its Eastern rivals.

"It was unbelievable," San Antonio Spurs center David Robinson said of the third-quarter shot. "I got out on the court and tried that. I couldn't even get the ball behind my back."

Bryant led the West team with 18 points in just 22 minutes of play. Jordan paced the Eastern squad with 23 points, dishing out eight assists despite playing with the flu. In the end, the Eastern Conference team played a fundamentally more solid game and won, 135-114. With his team down by double digits, Western Conference coach George Karl benched Bryant in the fourth quarter to let some of the other players play. Jordan was named game MVP for the third time in his Hall-of-Fame career.

The personal battle between the game's greatest player and his young challenger dominated conversations afterward, however.

"It was a good battle," declared Jordan. "It was a really fun game."

"It was Michael's day," Bryant said. "He's still the king."

The contest between the two high-flying guards had been built up in the newspapers for weeks. Not only was Kobe Bryant having an impressive second season for the Los Angeles Lakers, coming off the bench as the Lakers' "sixth man," but he was playing in a very Jordan-like manner. His high-flying dunks and explosive drives to the basket reminded many observers of the young Michael. Some even began to predict that Bryant's Lakers would dethrone Jordan's Bulls as NBA champions.

Meetings between the two teams had taken on a playoff intensity. In a December game in Chicago's United Center, Jordan and Bryant put on a memorable show. They matched each other shot for shot, with Jordan scoring 36 points and Bryant pouring in 33. The Bulls won 104-83. In another game, at Los Angeles's fabulous Forum just a week before All-Star Sunday, Jordan outscored Bryant 31 to 20, but the Lakers won 112-87.

Bryant made no secret of his admiration for Jordan. "I watch Michael and try to dissect his game," he said. "I try to step back and observe and learn."

Some of Bryant's All-Star teammates thought the youngster should have spent more time observing and less time showing off. Karl Malone of the Utah Jazz was especially peeved when Bryant waved him away so he could

Kobe Bryant goes to the basket while being guarded by Dikembe Mutombo in the first half of the 1998 NBA All-Star Game.

go one-on-one with a defensive player. And Western Conference coach George Karl pointed out that there is a fine line between exciting the fans and playing good basketball. "I thought we tried to be too entertaining," Karl said. "It's a team game. Kobe made some great plays, but Michael and the East made better basketball decisions."

Other players were more forgiving. "He's an eager guy with a lot of talent and energy all balled up," said the Sacramento Kings' Mitch Richmond of Bryant. "He wants to show his stuff."

Kobe Bryant is no stranger to criticism. Though he came into the All-Star Game averaging 17.8 points, there were some who said he was too young to play in an NBA All-Star Game—let alone start at guard against the great Michael Jordan. Some even said that the fans who voted him onto the squad were nothing more than teenagers in baggy pants who knew him only from his television commercials.

"I'm one of those baggy-pants teens," Bryant responded to his critics. "And I would have voted for me."

Despite all his doubters, Bryant finished second in fan voting to the Seattle Sonics' Gary Payton among Western Conference guards. Even Lakers coach Del Harris, who believed in bringing Bryant along slowly, said, "Kobe's going to be an All-Star for many years to come."

Bryant let his fans know he appreciated their support. "It's definitely cool, all those people who vote for me," he said. "It's good to know they support you, that they're out there responding to what you do."

The All-Star selection came one year earlier than Kobe Bryant thought it would. He had hoped to make the All-Star team by 1999, when the game would be played in his hometown of Philadelphia. But Kobe Bryant does a lot of things ahead of schedule, like leaping to the NBA straight out of high school in 1996. Or winning the slam dunk contest at the 1997 All-Star Game in Cleveland. And after his electrifying performance in the 1998 contest at Madison Square Garden, Bryant has proved that starting in the NBA, joining the ranks of the league's elite players, and leading his team to a championship are all matters of "when," not "if."

"Whenever it happens, it happens," said the latest star to be born on Broadway.

2

THE KID FROM PHILLY

As a three-year-old growing up in Philadelphia, Kobe Bryant knew exactly what he wanted to do for a living.

"Mom, I'm going to play in the NBA," he would tell his mother, Pam Bryant.

To most mothers, this would be nothing more than a boast. But Pam Bryant knew that Kobe had basketball in his blood. After all, Kobe's father, Joe "Jellybean" Bryant, did play in the NBA for the San Diego Clippers. And every time his game was on TV, little Kobe would set up his Nerf hoop in front of the television. He would wriggle his small body into a tiny NBA uniform and play along with the men on the screen. When Daddy made a basket, Kobe would make a basket. When Daddy took a gulp from his water bottle, Kobe took a swig out of his. And when Daddy would towel the sweat off his brow during the rest

Kobe Bryant's father, Joe Bryant, center, played professional basketball for 8 years in the NBA. Young Kobe idolized his dad and the game he played.

The Houston Rockets was one of the three teams Joe Bryant, Kobe's dad, (above left) played for in the NBA.

break between quarters, well, Kobe had that all taken care of as well.

"Mom, feel my neck. I'm sweating," Kobe would say, toweling himself off in the Bryant living room. Pam eventually had a basketball hoop put up behind their house so Kobe could practice somewhere other than the living room.

Both of Kobe's parents grew up in Philadelphia in close-knit families like the one they created for Kobe and his older sisters, Sharia and Shaya. They began dating after Pam attended one of Joe's LaSalle College basketball games. They were married seven months later—and soon took their marriage on the road to three NBA cities.

Joe Bryant played for eight years in the National Basketball Association, from 1975 to 1983, for the Philadelphia 76ers, then the San Diego Clippers, and finally for the Houston Rockets. His only son, Kobe, was born on August 23, 1978, in Philadelphia. When Joe's NBA career was over, he took a job playing in a European league. Kobe Bryant was only six when his family moved to Italy to be with their father. For the next eight years, the Bryants had to adapt to life in a foreign country. It was scary at first, learning how to deal with a different language, strange money, and a totally new culture. Kobe speaks perfect Italian today because of the time he spent living abroad. He also thinks the experience helped bring his family closer together.

"I think it's because we all grew up together in Italy. We didn't have anybody to depend on but our family," Kobe said. "We had to stick together."

Over time, the Bryants came to love Italy. They admired its people and their love of life. For Kobe, living in this ancient land was like a priceless education. On the playgrounds, he was schooled in the fundamentals of basketball in the European way. Off the court, he was able to broaden his horizons as well. His father felt the experience contributed to Kobe's later success.

"He has confidence as a human being and as a player," Joe Bryant said. "Being able to travel and see different cultures and different religions, I think, has made him a better human being. That's why he plays with such calm. He respects people, regardless of what they look like or what they do."

Kobe looks back fondly on the time he spent in Italy. In fact, he hopes one day to go there with his own wife and family.

"People treat others as equals there," he said. "They don't mistrust each other. They say hello when they see you on the street," he said. "And family, family is big there."

Family has always been a big part of Kobe Bryant's life. Someone once asked Kobe's mother what was the most important lesson she tried to teach her children. "Family first," she answered firmly. "Period. Family's absolutely first. I don't know any different."

Sports are a tradition in Kobe's family. Besides his father, his uncle John "Chubby" Cox also once played in the NBA and was a college star at Villanova University and the University of San Francisco. Kobe's sisters, Shaya, who is 6'4", and Sharia, who is 5'10", both excelled at volleyball, playing it in college. His mother, Pam, also 5'10", used to play street basketball.

"I hear she has a mean jump shot," said Kobe with a grin.

The family was always supportive of the athletic aspirations of all the Bryant children. At Kobe's basketball games, or at Shaya's or Sharia's volleyball matches, the immediate family was usually surrounded by a swarm of aunts, uncles, cousins, and neighbors cheering them on. It wasn't hard to bring them all together—most members of the Bryant-Cox extended family lived within a mile of one another.

"It's easy for you to keep your feet on the ground when you have the family that he has," said Kobe's Uncle Chubby.

Kobe knew how lucky he was to grow up in such a tight family. "I know I have it so lucky," he said. "I realize that there are kids growing up in a lot tougher situations than I am."

When Kobe was 14, his father's basketball career ended. The Bryant family left Italy and returned to Pennsylvania. Kobe remembered very little about the place he had left so long ago. Once again, he felt like a stranger in a foreign land—only this time the strange land was Lower Merion High School, near Philadelphia.

"It was pretty hard," he said. "I didn't know anybody. The school was just totally big."

As always, Kobe leaned on his family for support. One way of dealing with it was to focus on basketball. By this time, he and his father had become frequent one-on-one opponents.

"My father beat me up on the court," Kobe recalled. "He didn't do it to hurt me; he did it to make me tougher."

The more he practiced, the better he got. Kobe decided to go out for the Lower Merion varsity basketball team. With NBA dreams still on his mind, he turned to experts like Uncle Chubby to give him an idea of how good his game could become.

"It's not something he has to work at," Chubby observed. "It just comes natural. That's why he's going to make it. He's nurtured for it. He's ready for it. He's in full bloom."

Kobe was already thinking about the possibility that he would skip college and go directly to the pros. He even made a bet with a friend of his that he could pull it off. Only a few players in history, like the great center Moses Malone, had successfully made such a jump. Kobe was sure he could be one of them.

Kobe Bryant dunks the ball at Lower Merion High School, where he helped lead the team to the state championship.

Soon after returning from Italy, Kobe attended his first practice with the Lower Merion High School varsity basketball team. The coach, Gregg Downer, who had never seen him play before, was very impressed.

"I watched him for about five minutes," Downer said, "and then I turned to my assistants and said, 'This kid is going to be a pro.' That's how long it took for me to see that—five minutes."

As Kobe began his high school career, he knew he would be besieged by offers from college recruiters hoping to win him over with promises of scholarships. Such attention can be a big distraction for a young man trying to concentrate on his studies and improve his basketball skills. Once again, Kobe turned to his basketball family for advice and support.

Kobe's father had seen it all before. In 1972, he'd led his high school team to the Public League title. College recruiters began to call and visit him, trying to convince him to attend their schools. Before long, Joe Bryant was dizzy with the possibilities.

"It was a confusing time because my parents had never gone through this recruiting. I think my high school coach, he might have had one or two players prior, but this was relatively new to him, too," Joe Bryant recalled.

"It was just confusing because so many things were coming at you at one time. I think that was the problem. You didn't know who to believe, who to trust."

One thing Kobe was sure of was that it wasn't going to be that way for him. He had the experiences of his father and Uncle Chubby to draw on.

"They know. They know what it's like to play basketball," Kobe said.

3

ONE IN A MILLION

During the long, hot summers in Philadelphia, Kobe Bryant did not stray far from the game he loved. While his friends were at the beach, washing cars to earn a few dollars, or off on summer vacation, Kobe was still practicing in order to improve his game. He joined the Sonny Hill Summer League, a famous camp where instructors helped young players perfect their skills.

On his Sonny Hill application form, Kobe was asked to fill in his career goal. He saw no reason not to answer truthfully so he penciled in "NBA." The counselor who collected the forms was appalled.

"The guy said NBA players are one in a million," said Kobe. "I said, 'Man, look, I'm going to be that one in a million.'"

Kobe may have been confident, but he was not cocky. For his first three years at Lower Merion High School, he worked hard at his studies, paid attention at basketball practice, and looked to his coaches and teammates for advice. For most of that time, he led a fairly normal teenage

Kobe Bryant, left, played in the McDonald's All-American high school game in his senior year at Lower Merion High School in Pennsylvania.

life, unbothered by the crush of agents, scouts, and college recruiters. He was just Kobe Bryant, high school basketball player.

"I was the little man on campus," he recalled later. "Nobody recognized me or paid any attention to me. That gave me the opportunity to sneak in and do some positive things and learn from the people who were ahead of me." It would not always be this way for Kobe. Soon, he would not be able to hide under a cloak of anonymity.

The reason? His extraordinary play. Lower Merion had never had an athlete with Kobe's skills before. And his determination to succeed made him even better.

"He is blessed with a lot of natural ability and great genes, but the will is his and it's very strong," said Coach Gregg Downer. "Kobe has the skills and the maturity to be anything you could want."

There were some rough edges to his game. Sometimes, Kobe would dominate his opponents so much he would get bored. Instead of working on his mid-range jump shot, he would hoist the ball from long distances just to test his range. "Can we have a little 12-footer, not a 30-footer?" Coach Downer would yell at him.

More and more, it was Kobe's winning attitude that made him stand out among other talented players. Once he had the flu and was feeling terrible, but he insisted on playing because it was a big game. He sat on the far end of the Lower Merion bench with a towel around his aching head, separated from the other players so they wouldn't get sick. When he went into the game, he played brilliantly, as if nothing was wrong with him. Finally Kobe's mom replaced the sweaty towel with her own red shawl to keep him warm. And there he sat, all wrapped up in his mother's shawl.

"How many kids would do that?" Pam Bryant asked.

Kobe's leadership skills earned him respect in the Lower Merion locker room. "He's a motivator," said Rob Schwartz, one of Kobe's backups at guard. "He wasn't really much with pep talks, but when he spoke to you, you'd listen."

Kobe also led his teammates by example. During one game, his nose was broken in a collision with another player. His eye swelled up and he could barely see. Instead of coming out to get help for his injuries, he got up off the court and calmly sank a left-handed three-pointer with one eye closed. "Even though he was the best player on our team, he always worked hard," Schwartz observed.

Soon Kobe became something of a celebrity on the Lower Merion campus. When he would go to the gym to practice, other kids would gather around to get his autograph. Before long, nonstudents—not to mention agents and scouts—began lining up to get tickets to the Aces' basketball games. Still, Kobe's true friends did not treat him like royalty. To them, he was the same old Kobe.

"He's just a kid," said his friend Annie Schwartz. "For sure, he's not a Macaulay Culkin."

Kobe's spectacular play helped transform Lower Merion into a Pennsylvania powerhouse. His four-year totals broke the state high school career scoring record held by Wilt "the Stilt" Chamberlain. In his senior season, he averaged 31 points, 12 rebounds, seven assists, four blocks, and four steals a game. In the state finals, the Aces beat Eire Cathedral before a crowd of

With Lower Merion coach Gregg Downer looking on, Kobe signs autographs at the school gym. Kobe became a celebrity while still in high school.

Kobe presents Pennsylvania governor Tom Ridge with a school jersey at ceremonies for the state high school championship in 1996.

10,000 in the capital city of Harrisburg. For the first time in 53 years, they were Pennsylvania basketball champs.

Kobe had accomplished every goal a high school athlete could set for himself. But his biggest challenge lay ahead. He had to decide whether to go straight to the NBA or accept one of the many university scholarships being offered. To make his decision even tougher, he received a 1080 on his Scholastic Aptitude Tests (SAT). That score would earn him a spot in many good colleges, even if he didn't have great basketball skills.

Kobe thought it over long and hard. His mother expected him to attend college, but his gut instinct told him to make a stab at the pros. Over time, he convinced his parents that the time he spent in Europe was like a college education in itself. Maybe it was time he got a little graduate instruction in basketball, with the NBA as his alma mater.

"In that situation, I don't think there's a wrong

choice," said his father. "If you go to college and play basketball there, you meet people and on top of that, you get a good education. In the NBA, you're learning from the professionals and maturing as a person and as a basketball player, so the education factor is still there."

On Monday, April 29, 1996, Kobe announced his intentions. He called a meeting in the Lower Merion High School gym for 2:30 that afternoon. The whole school was on hand for a combination press conference and pep rally. Local reporters jostled for space with officials from ESPN and the major newspapers. Members of the pop group Boyz II Men were on hand to salute their fellow Philadelphian. Lower Merion's athletic director Tom McGovern called the gathering to order and introduced the featured speaker.

"In the last four years he's brought us joy, happiness, national recognition, and a state title," McGovern told the expectant throng. "We will be behind him 100 percent. We owe him that much." Then McGovern stepped aside and called Kobe to the podium.

Kobe wore a sport coat and slacks for the occasion, but he looked nervous and ill at ease as he approached the microphone. Saying good-bye to his friends and schoolmates was going to be difficult. Still, his mind was made up, and after rubbing his chin in contemplation for a moment he leaned forward and told the crowd:

"I've decided to skip college and take my talent to the NBA."

The crowd immediately exploded in a chorus of "Whoomp, there it is!" This was the news they were expecting to hear—and they were ecstatic. "Playing in the NBA has been my dream since I was three," Kobe continued. But he could bare-

Kobe's arrival at his senior prom with TV and singing star Brandy Norwood caused quite a sensation.

ly be heard above the din. The hard part was over, it seemed. Now he could get back to playing basketball.

There was one unfinished bit of high school business that Kobe wanted to attend to, however. That spring, at an All-Star basketball game in Philadelphia, Bryant met the girl of his dreams, Brandy. The singing sensation and star of the hit sitcom *Moesha* took an instant liking to him. Kobe soon worked up the nerve to ask her to his senior prom. To his delight, she accepted.

Lower Merion High had never seen anything like it. Kobe and Brandy arrived fashionably late—no doubt to fake out the swarms of reporters and photographers who had been alerted to the date. Brandy braided her hair and bought a new dress for the occasion. Kobe wore a tuxedo and band collar shirt with no tie. The couple walked hand-in-hand up a marble stairway to the second-floor ballroom as flashbulbs popped and fans cried out for autographs. Brandy's mother looked on nervously, anxious that her daughter have a good time amid the crush of media attention.

But this was no ordinary prom. It's not every day a high school basketball player arrives at the dance with one of *People Magazine*'s 50 Most Beautiful People. But Kobe Bryant's days as an everyday citizen were almost over. He was learning the life of a celebrity. And he liked it. The next day, he and Brandy headed off to Atlantic City for more celebration. Then Brandy flew home to California. Newspapers on both coasts heralded the arrival of the latest "power couple."

Having gotten his first taste of the Hollywood lifestyle, Kobe had only to secure his place in the NBA. The annual draft where teams select from among the best college, high school, and European players was coming up fast, on June 26th. Before then, there would be a series of informal workouts at which NBA prospects would show off their skills in front of NBA scouts and team executives. One team Kobe was especially interested in impressing was the Los Angeles Lakers.

Kobe had been a Lakers fan since childhood. He had watched Earvin "Magic" Johnson come up as a rookie and transform the NBA from a league of lumbering giants into a showtime spectacular dominated by dynamic guards. Kobe broke down crying the day he learned Magic had HIV and was retiring from basketball. The chance to play for the Lakers, one of basketball's prestigious franchises, filled Kobe with enthusiasm.

At a pre-draft workout, Lakers general manager Jerry West put Bryant through a rigorous battery of tests. Some tested his physical skills. West asked Bryant to jump, and Bryant responded by leaping so high he slapped the top of the backboard square. Other tests were designed to gauge Bryant's mental strength. West sent Bryant through an obstacle course with retired Laker Michael Cooper harassing him along the way. Cooper, a defensive specialist who was invariably assigned to guard Larry Bird in the NBA Finals, pushed and shoved Bryant, but the youngster refused to break under the pressure and completed the course. When the fun was over, West turned to his assistant and smiled.

"I've seen enough. Let's go," he said. Then the man whose image appears on the official NBA logo left the gym without another word. He would later call Bryant the best prospect he had ever put through a workout.

The promising workout gave Kobe some hope that the Lakers would draft him. However, if that was to happen, he would have to go undrafted by 23 other teams—not a likely prospect given all the media hype he was receiving. When draft day finally arrived, Kobe waited nervously in New Jersey's Continental Airlines Arena, with his mother squeezing his thigh and his sister squeezing his hand. Then, one by one, the names of the teams and the players they had drafted were read off by NBA commissioner David Stern.

Kobe's came 13th, when the Charlotte Hornets chose him with their first-round selection. While he knew it was coming, the sound of his name echoing from the microphones still hit him like a load of bricks.

"I heard the name Kobe, and then the cam-

Kobe Bryant, 17, whips his arm through the air as he exclaims that he'll do whatever he can to help the Los Angeles Lakers achieve a winning season after it was announced that the Lakers had signed him for a three-year contract.

eras started coming toward me, and I started thinking, 'Oh, man, yeah, I'm going to play in the NBA in about a minute.'"

Kobe met with the mob of reporters who descended upon him. "I'm very happy to be going to Charlotte," he said.

Before long, however, Kobe and his agent began to hear that he would not be a Hornet for long. Rumors were brewing that the Los Angeles Lakers were interested in trading for the rights to sign Kobe. They offered Charlotte center Vlade

Divac in exchange. For an agonizing week, Kobe's future was in limbo, as the two teams negotiated terms of a possible trade. Finally, when Divac gave his consent to the trade and agreed to leave his beloved Los Angeles, the matter was settled. Kobe Bryant was property of the L.A. Lakers.

"We're very excited to get a player with Kobe's talent and ability," said Jerry West. He claimed to be unconcerned about Kobe's youth and inexperience. "We feel his potential in this league is unlimited, but we'll be patient in letting him develop."

"This is a dream come true," Kobe said after the trade went through. "This is what I live for. It's the moment I've been waiting for."

He declared himself ready to participate in the summer rookie league to play himself into shape for the upcoming NBA season.

Before the summer was over, he signed a three-year contract worth $3.5 million. Now all he had to do was prove himself on the court, to show any doubters that he was worth all the hype.

Most experts believed that it was just a matter of time. Said NBA Hall-of-Famer Bob Lanier: "Kobe's got star written all over him."

4

GROWING PAINS

The Los Angeles Lakers entered the 1996-97 NBA season with high hopes. The previous year they had made the playoffs and were hailed as a young team on the rise. In the off-season, they had signed one of the game's premier big men, gargantuan center Shaquille O'Neal. The addition of Kobe Bryant made one of the NBA's youngest, most talented teams even better.

Bryant was eager to make an impression on the Laker coaches. But a couple freak injuries curtailed his progress. On September 2, he was playing a pickup game with some friends on Venice Beach. He went up for a layup and got fouled, put out his left hand to brace his fall, and ended up breaking his wrist. The injury kept Bryant from taking part in full-contact drills during training camp. Then in an October 19 exhibition game against the Philadelphia 76ers, Bryant was driving hard to the basket when he collided with Philly's Tim Kempton, injuring his lower back.

Laker coach Del Harris knew Bryant was trying hard to impress his new teammates, but he

Newly acquired by the Los Angeles Lakers, Kobe played in a summer league in July of 1996 to better prepare himself for the start of a professional career.

Kobe dribbles past Philadelphia 76er Allen Iverson, both considered to be among the most promising young athletes of the NBA.

cautioned him not to risk hurting himself by playing too aggressively. "You have to be selective when you expose yourself like that," Harris said.

The rough-and-tumble style was nothing new to Bryant, however. "I'm kind of used to it," he said. "In high school, it happened about every play." Nevertheless, he agreed with his coach that it was important to draw fouls in crucial moments. "There are situations in games when you know what you need," Bryant said. "You might need to get to the free throw line or whatever, so you try for the contact. You've just got to pick the situations."

The bumps and bruises may have prevented Bryant's coaches from getting a handle on his abilities, but they did not affect his off-the-court development. He signed a contract with Adidas to endorse their shoes and joined the Screen Actors Guild to kick start his acting career. He appeared in guest-starring roles on the TV comedy series *Arli$$* (with pudgy punchinello Robert Wuhl) and *Moesha* (with his old friend Brandy).

For Bryant, it was an opportunity to learn about other aspects of life besides sports. "I like getting out there and having a good time and meeting people," he said of his endorsement and entertainment appearances. "I like to see the end product, and I take pride in it. I want my product to be one of the best things out there. And I love going in front of the cameras and learning something new. But I understand basketball is what got me here, and on top of that, I love to do it so much that it will always be my focal point."

Some rookies would have been distracted by all this attention, but not Kobe.

"It's crazy," he said. "If you sit back and start thinking about it, maybe you could be overwhelmed by the situation. You've just got to keep going slowly and keep working hard on your basketball skills. Then, I don't think your head can swell because you won't have time to think about it."

Other than buying clothes for his sisters, however, Bryant did not spend his newfound endorsement riches. He claimed not to have the patience for shopping sprees. He made only one luxury purchase—an ocean-front house in the Pacific Palisades for himself and his entire family. His parents and sister Shaya promptly joined him on the West Coast, while Sharia remained behind to finish her senior season with the Temple volleyball team. The presence of his family meant that Bryant would stay grounded and not let the many distractions of Hollywood go to his head.

By the time the NBA season began, Bryant had missed almost five weeks of training camp due to his various injuries. Nevertheless he took the court as scheduled on Sunday, November 3, 1996, at home against the Minnesota Timberwolves. When he came off the bench at the 2:47 mark of the first quarter, he became the youngest man ever to play in an NBA game, at age 18. For openers, it was a pretty good night. He got in six minutes of playing time, missed his only shot, grabbed one rebound, blocked a shot, and had one turnover. Best of all, the Lakers won 91-85.

After the game, Bryant could celebrate his accomplishment. "I guess it's pretty nice because a lot of guys come into the NBA," he said. "It'll be neat one day to sit with my grandkids and tell them I was the youngest player in NBA history. By then, somebody may be coming out of middle school."

Bryant's achievement was impressive. It was not the start of a blistering run of NBA successes, however. Along with his injuries, Bryant's progress was hampered further by a hectic November schedule that had the Lakers playing almost every other night. As a result, Bryant didn't get a chance to practice much with the team. He had to learn all their plays on the fly, during regular season games. He also found his notoriety could be a hindrance, because opposing teams spent so much effort scouting the player some were calling "the next Michael Jordan."

Frustration began to set in. Bryant averaged

only 5.3 points over his first 25 games. He sank less than 40 percent of his shots and spent all but 10 minutes of every contest on the bench. Still, he couldn't complain, as strong play by the rest of the Los Angeles reserves propelled the team to an 18-7 record.

Despite Bryant's slow start, his supporters weren't worried. "Certainly, Kobe's development has been hampered to a degree by the injuries and the missed training camp," said Lakers general manager Mitch Kupchak. "But when you take a step back and maybe compare him to the other high school players who have gone right to the NBA, there's not much more to say about what he could be doing."

The Lakers treated Bryant like a star pupil in the school of professional basketball. To spur his development, they even provided him with a tutor. Byron Scott, the 35-year-old veteran of past Laker championship teams, rejoined the team to provide a role model for the young guard. The sweet-shooting Scott advised Bryant to keep practicing and be ready to play every day.

"Byron told me how important it is during the season to keep your work habits," Bryant said. "You have to keep working on your jump shot, your physical preparation. At this level, you always have to be working to improve your game or you'll get left behind."

By the start of the New Year, all that preparation had begun to pay off. Bryant's play improved to the point that he was now a valuable contributor from the Laker bench. At times he was even allowed to direct the team's offense, spelling veteran Nick Van Exel at the point guard position. Along with the other top rookies in the NBA, he was invited to Cleveland in February to participate in the annual All-Star festivities.

The atmosphere was electrifying. Bryant met the NBA's great players, compared notes with other rookies, and sought advice from some of the legends of basketball. Earl "the Pearl" Monroe spotted Bryant and told him to keep working hard and stay prepared.

"Coming from him, that was something special," Bryant said.

Seeing stars was only part of the All-Star festivities, however. There were also a number of exhibition games and skills contests. Bryant's first competition was the rookie game, held the Friday before the All-Star Game. His Lakers teammates and fellow first-year players Travis Knight and Derek Fisher joined him on the Western Conference team. As usual, Bryant was anything but shy. He came out shooting, hoisting up 12 shots in the first half. In the second half, he switched to the dribble drive, earning 13 trips to the free throw line and converting on 12 of them. He led all scorers in the game with 31 points, but the East beat his Western squad, 96-91. When it came time to choose the game's Most Valuable Player, the crowd cheered for Bryant. But the voters chose the Philadelphia 76ers' dynamic point guard, Allen Iverson.

Bryant moved on to the Slam Dunk Contest, competing against not only other rookies but veterans as well. He was only five when the first NBA Slam Dunk Contest took place in 1984. Winning the competition in his first year was a daunting prospect for a player who made his first dunk ever only three years before, in the Lower Merion High School gym. And that one was something less than spectacular.

"It really wasn't a dunk," Bryant recalled. "It

Bryant slam dunks a ball in the style that won him the Slam Dunk Contest in his first NBA All-Star Game.

was one of those things where you grab the rim and the ball happens to go in. But after that I was really excited. I was really hyped up and dunking was something I worked on."

In 1996, Bryant entered his first-ever slam dunk competition, a contest for high school players conducted in Myrtle Beach, South Carolina. Now, just a year later, he was set to go up against some of the best leapers and jammers in the NBA. Instead of panicking, he took a deep breath and remembered his father's words of advice: "If you miss, don't worry about it, we love you, anyway."

The contest began with a preliminary round, after which only the most spectacular dunkers would move on to the finals. Bryant earned his spot in the finals with a thunderous jam in which he double-pumped, brought the ball down between his legs, and put home a reverse. He modeled the move on an Isaiah Rider jam from the 1994 competition. His opponents in the final round were Chris Carr of the Minnesota Timberwolves and Michael Finley of the Dallas Mavericks. Bryant would need to come up with a real show stopper if he had any chance of winning.

Finley's first attempt in the finals was a miss, but it may have been the most spectacular attempt of the night. He started on the left, threw the ball high in the air, and then did a cartwheel on his way to the hoop. He got the ball in mid-air but failed to slam it home. Finley still scored a 33 out of 50, but when he failed on his next attempt he was all but eliminated.

Carr hit both of his slams in the final round. Both shots were high tosses that he picked up off the bounce and slammed through the nylon cord. They were solid slams, but the highest score awarded to him by the judges was a 45. Bryant sensed that victory was within his reach.

For his first dunk of the finals, Bryant started at halfcourt to get a running start. As he drove the lane, he executed a breathtaking between-the-legs move and soared to the basket. After he jammed the ball cleanly through the net, he lingered underneath the hoop to flex his muscles and admire his handiwork. In the stands, his prom date Brandy led a chorus of whoops from the pumped-up fans. The judges awarded Bryant 49 out of a possible 50 points. With this almost perfect jam, he eliminated Finley and Carr to claim the slam dunk title.

Afterward, Bryant was ecstatic. "That's something I've always dreamed about doing since I was a little kid," he crowed.

After the excitement of All-Star weekend, Kobe Bryant returned to the grind of the regular-season NBA schedule. February and March are known as the "dog days" of the season, because the cold weather, constant travel, and fatigue have players eager to get the playoffs underway. It is also the point in the season when rookie players get worn down by the length of the 82-game NBA season compared to the shorter college or high school schedule. The fatigue is referred to as "hitting the wall."

Bryant not only failed to hit the wall, he did his best to leap over it. Pumped up with confidence after his All-Star weekend performance, he showed none of the weariness that many other NBA players have come to accept as the first sign of spring.

"It's fun," he told reporters in mid-season. "I'm in the NBA. No way I'm bored. In four years, then I'll probably be like, 'Oh God, We've got another road trip.' Right now, it's great."

Whenever he could, Bryant compared notes on the rookie experience with other first-year players. Jermaine O'Neal, a forward with the Portland Trailblazers who had also jumped straight from high school to the pros, became a trusted confidant. And after every home game, Bryant returned to his six-bedroom beach house

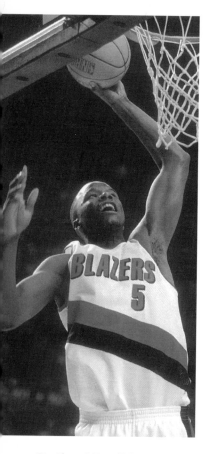

Portland Trailblazer Jermaine O'Neal was next in line to Kobe as the two youngest players in the NBA. He and Kobe became friends with this common bond.

to shoot pool and talk things over with his father. These contacts helped Bryant deal with the difficulties of life in the NBA.

Bryant also drew inspiration from a historical source. "I read the autobiography of Jackie Robinson," he said. He learned about how the man who broke Major League Baseball's color barrier had to endure taunts and threats from players and fans across the country. "I was thinking about all the hard times I'd go through this year, and that it'd never compare to what he went through. That just kind of helped put things in perspective."

Amazingly, Bryant found it harder to adjust to life on the court than off it. One of the hardest things for Bryant was not knowing whether he was going to play or how many minutes he would get on the floor. On several occasions, he was pulled from games by Coach Del Harris for not playing "in the flow" of the Lakers offense. Also, because Bryant was still growing (he spurted from 6'5" to 6'6" over the course of the season), Harris did not always know where to play his talented rookie. Bryant saw time at point guard, shooting guard, and even small forward. This made it tougher for him to fit in and learn his role on the team.

Bryant was eager to earn more playing time and show his fans what he could do. "You can only learn so much by watching," he remarked. Backing Bryant in his request for more minutes was the Lakers president Jerry West, himself a former NBA star, who let Del Harris know the rookie should be on the court more. Reluctantly Harris agreed, and Bryant finished the season averaging 15.5 minutes, 7.6 points, 1.3 assists, and 1.9 rebounds in 71 regular-season games.

It was a solid contribution to a team that needed a boost from its bench players. Center Shaquille O'Neal and forward Robert Horry missed significant portions of the season because of injuries, forcing others to pick up the slack. Fortunately, the Lakers had found some rookie gems in Travis Knight and Derek Fisher and were able to hold the fort until the hobbled starters returned. They finished with 57 wins, good enough for second place in the NBA's Pacific Division. The opening round of the playoffs saw Los Angeles matched up against Jermaine O'Neal and the Portland Trailblazers.

That test proved easy to pass, as the explosive Lakers blitzed the punchless Blazers three games to one. Then it was on to Salt Lake City, and a seven-game tilt with one of the NBA's deepest teams, the Utah Jazz. Power forward Karl Malone (known as the Mailman because he "always delivers") led the charge for the Jazz, which also featured the sweet-shooting backcourt tandem of John Stockton and Jeff Hornacek. Many observers believed that the winner of this series would go on to represent the Western Conference in the NBA Finals.

The Jazz took the first two contests on its home floor. The Lakers then rallied before a pumped-up Forum crowd to capture Game Three, 104-84. They gave a disappointing effort in the next game, however, and were blown out of their own gym, 110-95. The series now headed back to Utah, where the Lakers faced elimination before a jubilant Delta Center crowd.

It was to be a classic playoff struggle. This time Los Angeles came with maximum effort, showing the kind of heart and determination even the team's most loyal fans had begun to doubt. Shaquille O'Neal scored 23 points and hauled in 13 rebounds to pace the Laker attack, while guard Nick "the Quick" Van Exel rode a second-half hot streak to score 26. But the Jazz seemed to match them shot for shot. The Mailman delivered 32 points of his own to lead all scorers, with the pesky Stockton handing out assists.

The game was close deep into the fourth quarter of play. The teams traded baskets down the stretch and were knotted at 87-87 with less than a minute left. When Van Exel stripped the ball from center Greg Ostertag with 11.3 seconds remaining, the Lakers had one last chance to win the game in regulation. Del Harris called a time-out to set up a final play.

The Lakers had time for only one shot. But who should take it? The coach's options were severely limited. Shaquille O'Neal had committed his sixth foul and was disqualified from the game. Robert Horry had been ejected by the officials for shoving Jeff Hornacek. And guard Eddie Jones and forward Elden Campbell were each having terrible nights offensively. Harris's choice came down to Van Exel or Kobe Bryant. While Van Exel was playing a great game, Harris had seen enough of Kobe's one-on-one skills to know he could torch the Jazz defenders.

"Kobe can get his shot any time he wants," Harris reasoned. "He's 18, but you can't guard him."

When the teams returned to the floor, Kobe Bryant had the ball in his hands. As he brought it upcourt, the Lakers spread across the floor to allow him the room he needed to pick his shot. Utah's Bryon Russell closed in to defend Bryant, who waited the entire 11 seconds before pulling up from 14 feet out to hoist a jump shot. With

Russell's long arms in his face, Bryant couldn't get a clear look at the rim, but there were no excuses for such an erratic shot. It missed the basket entirely for an embarrassing air ball as the buzzer sounded. Bryant had failed. The game was going to overtime.

"Bryon Russell wasn't going to let some 18-year-old show him up on national TV," Karl Malone railed.

The Jazz continued to play the "Stop Kobe" defense in the overtime period. While Nick Van Exel failed to take a single shot, Bryant missed on four of five opportunities. Three of them were air balls, causing the frenzied Utah crowd to taunt him mercilessly. The Mailman came up big, by contrast, with six points in the extra session to lead the Jazz to a 98-93 series-clinching win.

After the game, the talk was all about Bryant's failure.

"Tonight, I just didn't come through," he said afterward. "But play the game again, and I want the ball again."

Many questioned Harris's strategy. Why give the ball to a rookie playing in only his second NBA playoff series—and an 18-year-old rookie at that? Among those sniping at the coach's decision was Nick Van Exel.

"I felt I wanted to take the last shot, but he wanted to go to Kobe," said the disgruntled guard.

Even some of the Jazz players were surprised by Harris's actions.

"Nick was having a heckuva game, but I guess that's why I'm not a coach," said "Mailman" Karl Malone.

For his part, Del Harris remained unfazed by the controversy. He even found it ironic, con-

sidering the abuse he had suffered from some of the same critics throughout the season.

"I spent over half of the year being criticized for not playing Kobe," Harris cracked. "Now I'm getting criticized for playing him."

The Utah Jazz went on to defeat the Houston Rockets in the Western Conference Finals. They were beaten in the NBA Finals in a hard-fought series with the Chicago Bulls, four games to three. Missing those shots against the Jazz might have denied Kobe Bryant a spot on basketball's biggest stage, against its greatest player, Michael Jordan. It was a disappointment the young star would not soon forget.

Kobe Bryant's first season in the NBA was now history. Like a lot of other rookie campaigns, it had been filled with ups and downs. The play-off loss to Utah was just the final lesson in a year-long learning experience. Now it was up to Bryant to use what he had learned to take his game to the next level. That process started almost immediately.

A few days after the playoffs ended, a reporter asked Bryant how much time he planned to take off before getting back on the court to get ready for the next season.

"A couple of days," he replied. "I've still got a lot of energy left, man."

Kobe loses the ball as Utah Jazz forward Antoine Carr falls to the floor in the 1997 playoffs.

5

THE TEAM OF THE FUTURE

True to his word, Kobe Bryant returned to the UCLA gym just a few hours after the Lakers' team plane had returned from Utah. There he found a surprise visitor—Magic Johnson. The ex-Laker great was proud to see his young charge so eager to get back into the practice groove after such a devastating loss.

"That was just like me," beamed Magic. "I loved seeing that from him. That's how I reacted, too. This is where he needs to be."

There was now just one final task to perform before he could clear out the cobwebs for the new season. He had to watch the film of his Game Five flame-out against the Jazz. Where most players would have cried, however, Kobe Bryant just laughed. He found it comical that he had missed such an easy opportunity to ice the game. And he made a promise to himself that it would never happen again.

Kobe leaves the arena with a big smile after helping the Lakers defeat the Seattle SuperSonics. Kobe began the 1997-98 season sporting a new Afro hair-do.

Before the 1997-98 campaign began, Bryant made the first of many changes he hoped would allow him to assert his personality more forcefully in his second season. He showed up at training camp with a new haircut, an Afro that recalled the glory days of basketball in the 1970s.

"When I came to the Lakers last year, I wanted to get a clean start," Bryant explained of the new hairdo. "But this year, this is me."

His Laker teammates needled him a bit about the crazy hairstyle, but Bryant took it all in stride.

"My parents raised me to be an individual," he remarked. "The key to success at anything, I think, is avoiding peer pressure."

Bryant did draw the line at some fashion statements popular with young players, however, like tattoos—and especially earrings.

"I don't want holes in my ears," he told reporters. "Nothing against anybody else, but it's not for me."

Whether it was the new lid, the extra practice, or just natural development, Kobe came out smoking to start the 1997-98 season. Again spending time at three positions, he found it easier to break into Del Harris's playing rotation and got a rhythm going offensively. By the All-Star break, he was averaging almost 17 points a game as a bench player and earning favorable press for his willingness to learn team basketball.

"Kobe Bryant has matured dramatically," said Indiana Pacers president Donnie Walsh. "I think he understands his role much more. Instead of just showing what he can do, he is playing winning basketball."

He also had redemption on his mind. In the Lakers' first visit to the Delta Center since los-

The Chicago Bulls' Michael Jordan tries to maneuver around Bryant in the 1997 All-Star game in Chicago.

ing to Utah in the playoffs, Bryant showed what he had learned by blocking Bryon Russell's three-point shot attempt in the game's final seconds. Then he ran the length of the floor for a thunderous dunk that sealed the game for the Lakers. With plays like that, people started calling him "the next Michael Jordan."

The plays also earned him a spot on the All-Star team. But after his memorable weekend in Manhattan, Bryant found it hard to readjust to life as an everyday player. He tried to live up to his hype and as a result his game struggled. Over one 24-game stretch, he made only 37 percent of his shots. His scoring average fell almost six points per game. Some of his teammates began to whisper that he was being too selfish on the court. In order to teach Bryant a lesson about team play, Del Harris reduced his playing time by almost seven minutes a contest. Once a favorite for the "Sixth Man Award" given annually to the most productive reserve, Bryant now seemed a longshot to win that honor.

As the playoffs neared, however, Harris began to put aside his reservations and insert Bryant into the lineup more frequently. He knew that the Lakers needed him for the post-season run. If Bryant was rusty or if his confidence was shattered by his poor play and lack of court time, he would carry those traits over into the playoff tournament. And that would spell disaster for a Los Angeles squad that needed his explosive offense in crunch time.

When the regular season ended in late April, Bryant had put together what looked on paper like a very successful season. He upped his averages in virtually every important offensive category, averaging 15.4 points in 26 minutes per game. But he had really had two seasons: the torrid pre-All-Star stretch in which he had taken the league by storm and the shaky second half in which he had tried to do too much, too quickly. Now he needed to have a good playoff to prove he belonged with the NBA's elite.

So did the Los Angeles Lakers. After spending two years as the NBA's Next Great Team, they were eager to fulfill their potential and make it to the finals. They knew they had a good shot if they could get there. The Chicago Bulls seemed old and vulnerable, and the Lakers' 60-22 record proved they were among the dominant teams in

Kobe aims for the hoop against the defense of Portland's Brian Grant during a first-round playoff game.

the hunt to replace the Bulls as champions. As a result, Bryant and the Lakers stormed into their first-round match-up with Portland showing a newfound ferocity.

Bryant saw early action in Game One at the Forum. He drained his first shot, a 17-footer over the Trailblazers Isaiah "J.R." Rider, but struggled after that. He spent the first half hoisting up ill-advised shots and finished making only one out of four from the field. As the game went on, however, Bryant opted for a change of approach.

"I wanted to come out with a big fourth quarter," he said. He decided to junk his jump shot and instead began driving to the basket, using powerful screens from big man Shaquille O'Neal to blow by Portland defenders.

"I knew I could penetrate," Bryant explained. "I knew I could find some gaps here and there."

One of the men trying unsuccessfully to guard him was Rasheed Wallace, a burly forward against whom Bryant had played while at Lower Merion.

"Me and Rasheed have been going at each other since high school," Bryant said later. "We're pretty used to that matchup."

Bryant finished the game with an offensive flurry. He scored 11 points over the final 12 minutes to propel the Lakers to a 104-102 victory. During timeouts, he thought back to the Game Five loss in Utah for inspiration. This time the end result was more to his liking.

"After the buzzer went off and we had a two-point lead, I was like, 'Ah, good job, man. Now you can sleep tonight.'"

In the second game, Bryant scored only four points as the Lakers turned to their other players for offensive punch. But the team won, 108-99, and the second-year guard wasn't complaining.

"We're not a one-man show," he told interviewers. "The other night, they weren't keying on me, so I took full advantage by going to the cup. Today could have been the same, but other guys were open. Other guys had the hot hand."

It was a lesson the Lakers had waited a long time for their young phenom to learn. Playing within the team framework allowed Kobe and the Lakers to finish the Trailblazers in four games. In the decisive contest, Bryant finished with 22 points, including a dramatic dunk in the fourth quarter that made highlight films across the country.

Next up for the Lakers were the mighty Seattle SuperSonics, an explosive team that had beaten them out for the Pacific Division title in the regular season. It seemed as if that trend would continue in Game One, as Seattle used the three-point shot to take the opener, 106-92. Bryant was not much of a factor in that game, and he was even less of a factor in the next two, as a flu bug kept him sidelined for two Los Angeles victories.

The team's dramatic turnaround prompted some observers to conclude that Los Angeles was a better team without their high-flying guard on the floor. Nick Van Exel, it was said, played a much more relaxed game without fear that Bryant would replace him in the lineup at any moment.

"They don't even miss him," observed a laconic Sam Perkins, a Sonics center. "It seems like they are more at ease without him."

Other players thought differently. "If we're fortunate enough to move to the next series, Kobe will be an important player for us," said Laker guard Derek Fisher. "We definitely want him back."

Bryant did return for Game Four but played only three minutes in a 112-100 Laker romp. Back in Seattle for Game Five, the Lakers seized the chance to close out their hated rivals with a

Portland's Rasheed Wallace dunks the ball over the head of Laker Nick Van Exel.

Kobe attempts to get around the defense of Utah Jazz guard Jeff Hornacek.

110-95 thrashing. Kobe contributed seven points in 11 minutes off the bench.

The Lakers now had an opportunity to reach their goal of making the NBA finals. All that stood in the way was one of the best teams of the 1990s, their old enemies the Utah Jazz. But this time there would be no chance for a last-second shot for Kobe. In a stunning turn of events, the Jazz wiped out the Lakers in four straight games, including an embarrassing clinching victory on Los Angeles's own home floor. The Lakers high hopes of assuming dominion over the Western Conference crumbled in the face of the Utah onslaught.

Each Laker played a part in the debacle. After scoring 16 points in Game One, Bryant was held to single digits in the remaining contests. He shot a poor percentage from the floor and was beaten like a drum defensively. But then so were all of the Lakers, as they seemed to have no response to the Jazz's elegant, machine-like offense. The loss left the Lakers dumbfounded. Management promised there would be changes made in the off-season.

Just as he had the previous summer, Bryant got right back into the gym to prepare for another season. One of his favorite drills is a game he invented himself. He calls it "shadow basketball."

"I play against my shadow," he explained.

Ultimately, trying to catch up with his own potential will be Kobe Bryant's biggest challenge. If he does so, he will earn a starting assignment and from there take his team to an NBA title. To accomplish these goals, he will have to raise his level of play even further. He will have to learn how to lead while still playing within the confines of team basketball.

Graduating to the next level is never easy. When you join the NBA right out of high school, you have to pick up things on the fly that others have the luxury of four years of college to learn. But that is the path Kobe Bryant chose.

Utah's Karl Malone shoots over the long reach of Kobe Bryant.

He is as aware of its difficulties as he is of its rewards.

"Basketball is kind of like life," he once said. "It can get rough at times. You can get knocked on your butt a couple of times. But what you have to do is get up and hold your head high and try again. That's how I'm going to do it. I'm sure there are times guys are knocking me on my butt and pushing me and I might start bleeding, but I have to get back up and keep going."

CHRONOLOGY

1978   Born August 23, 1978, in Philadelphia

1984   Family moves to Italy

1991   Family moves back to the United States

1996   Leads Lower Merion High School to Pennsylvania state championship; selected by *USA Today* and *Parade Magazine* as the National High School Player of the Year; announces his intention to skip college and enter the NBA draft; selected 13th in NBA draft by the Charlotte Hornets; traded to the Los Angeles Lakers for center Vlade Divac; becomes the youngest player ever to appear in an NBA game, against the Minnesota Timberwolves on November 3

1997   Scores 12 points in his first career start against the Dallas Mavericks on January 28, 1997; wins the Nestle Crunch Slam Dunk during the 1997 NBA All-Star weekend; scores a season-high 24 points against the Golden State Warriors on April 8, 1997; named to the 1996-97 NBA All-Rookie Second Team

1998   Finishes second in Western Conference All-Star voting to Seattle's Gary Payton; starts in All-Star Game

STATISTICS

KOBE BRYANT

NBA Regular Season

Season/Team	G	MPG	FGM	FGA	Pct	FTM	FTA	Pct	REB	AST	PTS	AVG
96-97 Lakers	71	15.5	176	422	.417	136	166	.819	132	91	539	7.6
97-98 Lakers	79	26.0	391	913	.428	363	457	.794	242	199	1220	15.4
TOTALS	150	21.1	567	1335	.425	499	623	.801	374	290	1759	11.7

G	games	FTA	free throws attempted
MPG	minutes per game	REB	rebounds
FGM	field goals made	AST	assists
FGA	field goals attempted	PTS	points
Pct	percentage	AVG	scoring average
FTM	free throws made		

FURTHER READING

Green, Ron, Jr. "Kobe Bryant Isn't Your Average 17-year-old." Knight-Ridder/Tribune News Service, June 27, 1996.

Lelyveld, Nita. "For High School Phenom Kobe Bryant, It's a Family Affair." Knight-Ridder/Tribune News Service, April 7, 1996.

Plaschke, Bill. "Mr. Excitement." *The Sporting News*, December 8, 1997.

Smallwood, John. "Kobe Suffers from Lack of Exposure in Los Angeles." Knight-Ridder/Tribune News Service, July 12, 1996.

Tresniowski, Alex. "Boy Wonder." *People Weekly*, March 31, 1997.

ABOUT THE AUTHOR

Robert Schnakenberg is an author and sports fan from New York City. He has written biographies of Scottie Pippen, Karl Malone, John Stockton, and Derek Jeter. He roots for the Yankees and Knicks.

INDEX

PHOTO CREDITS
AP/Wide World Photos: pp. 2, 8, 10, 12, 14, 16, 20, 22, 25, 26, 27, 29, 32, 34, 36, 41, 44, 48, 50, 53, 55, 57, 58, 60